An Interview with God

STEPHANIE HILL NCHEGE

ISBN 978-1-64079-589-1 (Paperback)
ISBN 978-1-64079-590-7 (Digital)

Copyright © 2017 by Stephanie Hill Nchege
All rights reserved. No part of this publication may be reproduced, distributed, or transmitted in any form or by any means, including photocopying, recording, or other electronic or mechanical methods without the prior written permission of the publisher. For permission requests, solicit the publisher via the address below.

Christian Faith Publishing, Inc.
296 Chestnut Street
Meadville, PA 16335
www.christianfaithpublishing.com

Printed in the United States of America

I dedicate this book to my mother, Veronica Hill. You taught me to study, to listen, and to cherish the value in being called for an interview with God. You have been my brightest light on earth. You exemplify daily what a woman after God's heart looks like. I love you.

Introduction

Imagine God having the angel Gabriel to call you and set up an interview. Gabriel tells you that God has a great position open, and that God, the big boss himself, is certain that you will be a great candidate. He then tells you that your interview process will begin tomorrow, and then he hangs up the phone. How would you respond? Would you think, *This can't be real?* Would you start getting out your best clothes, maybe you would start praying all day and all night, perhaps you'd start reading the Bible and memorizing scriptures. Who would you tell? Anyone? Would you be excited, nervous, or afraid? Do you think that you'd show up a couple of hours early for the interview or play it cool?

It may seem like a strange thought to even ponder because maybe you are thinking that God would never call you for an interview. But I believe that God sets up interviews every day. Think about it, when Moses had his interview, he started telling God that he didn't speak very well. Jonah actually got offered a position and decided to leave town. Queen Esther had a very frightening interview but decided she'd accept the position and dressed in her finest garments for the position. However we respond and prepare for our interview with God, I believe that there is one thing for certain, and that is that the questions that God will ask and the dialogue that we will have with him will change us forever.

Throughout this book, we will explore questions that God might ask us during our interview process as well as ones that you've probably asked God at some point in your life. In this book I've shared a few excerpts from biblical interviews as well as interview accounts that have happened in my own personal life, and there is also an interview shared from an amazing friend of mine that we shall call Jennifer, as it is her desire to share her story while remaining anonymous. Each chapter except the first is titled with an interview question. I hope that you will ponder and reflect upon each question for your life and write down your own answers for each.

I believe that questions are powerful tools that can help us to map out our visions that God has for our lives. Questions help us to identify the answers that lie inside of our hearts. And I believe that it is those answers that unlock our purpose, the mysteries of our heart, and deepen our relationship and walk with God. It is my prayer that as you read each chapter, the questions posed and the short stories used as answers in mine and other people's lives will encourage and motivate you to look forward to your own personal heart-to-heart interview with God.

1
Heart-to-Heart Interview with God

Do you remember the game 21 Questions? It's a very simple game where you get to ask another person twenty-one questions; usually these questions are yes or no closed-ended questions, but over the years, depending on the setting of where the game is being played, the objective can differ. 21 Questions has been played as icebreakers in company meetings, in small-group settings to get to know a colleague better, and my most favorite is when we used to play it as kids on long road trips when we were bored. Regardless of where the game is played or whether the questions are closed-ended or open-ended, the *results* never change. By the time you are finished with the series of questions, you have gotten to know the other person better, and usually, that's a great place to begin building a connection.

I want you to imagine that throughout the rest of this book, you and God are having an interview. This is a very unique interview because it will last for at least fourteen days. Each day, I pray that you will come back eager and excited to continue the conversation. The objectives of this interview are twofold. First, during the interview, you and God will get to know one another better. Second, you will begin to speak and live as if the things that he tells you are real and true for your life because they are. We don't live by the circumstances around us, but instead by the truth spoken by God that lives inside of us. During this interview, it is crucial that you listen to God's voice.

As you are preparing for this interview comprised of heart-to-heart matters, I want you to pause for a moment and think about what God's voice sounds like. Does it sound like James Earl Jones, maybe Morgan Freeman? I know, how about Charlton Heston? Oh wait, that was Moses in the movie *Ten Commandments* (just a little joke). But seriously, during this interview, it's okay to stop and have reflective moments, and I also hope that you will have a few transforming moments as well.

Now, let's think back to God's voice. I know that you've heard it before. Think about what it sounded like. Perhaps you heard it when you were on your knees in prayer, or maybe it was heard during a time when there was a softness that spoke to you and said, "Be still" or "It's okay. I'm with you." Whatever that time was in your life when you know with absolute certainty that you heard God speak to you, I want you to focus in on hearing that same voice as you begin this interview.

Now that you are keenly aware of what his voice sounds like, next, I want you to think about what does God have on? Just indulge me for a moment with this exercise. I want you to fully engage your senses as you experience the fullness of God throughout this interview process. Moses was afraid to look upon him at the burning bush, but you don't have to be afraid to see him, hear him, and even touch him. He is just as excited as you are to have this time with you. Look at him again as you are entering into this interview. Is he dressed in his Kingship Garment with a long white robe and crown of glory upon his head, or maybe he is sitting in his Son Ship clothing as a battered servant who hung upon the cross wearing torn clothing, having bloodstained hands, and wearing a crown of thorns upon his head? See him; take every bit of his presence in as you begin to talk heart-to-heart matters with him.

As you are listening to God's voice and looking at your savior, how do you feel? Do you want to lie in his arms like a child who is talking to their father with a blessed assurance that they are loved and protected? Maybe you feel like a servant, who is not worthy to even sit across from and get instruction from their master as you are looking upon his majestic face. However you feel right now as you are thinking about God's presence and what his voice is going to sound like as he speaks to your heart, I want you to remember this: He can only speak truth. He can only have a conversation with you that has "plans to prosper you and not to harm you, plans to give you hope and a future " (Jer. 29:11, NIV).

Who Do You Say I Am?

Now that you've prepared your heart and gotten ready, it's time to begin the interview. The first question is one that God is asking you. He wants to know, *Who do you say I am?* In two of the Gospels, Matthew 16:15 and Mark 8:29, there is a recording of this very question being posed to Jesus's closest disciples. Isn't it odd that this question is being asked by Jesus to the people who were the closest to him? Why would he ask them such a question? Surely, if anyone knew who he was, it would be his closest friends. Right?

Have you ever thought about your answer to this question? Fill your name in the blank as God is asking you, "_____, who do you say I am?" In order to help you answer this question, I want you to think about when you were first introduced to him. Were you a young child listening to your grandmother sing a hymnal? Maybe she was singing, "Are You Washed in the Blood?" Maybe your introduction came during a church service that you didn't even want to attend, and the preacher spoke about this God that had sent his son to die for your sins because he so loved you.

I can remember my first introduction to God. I was seven years old, and I was at a revival service. It was a Friday night. The evangelist for the week, Min. Johnnie J. Reed, was preaching about this God who didn't want anyone to be lost, but instead this God wanted all to live in paradise with him. He wanted us to live in mansions on streets made of gold, and the gates are made of pearl. Then I can remember Minister Reed asking if there was anyone who wanted to know this God and prepare their life to spend eternity with him? I remember at that moment getting up and running to the altar. I was the first one there. I remember how those tears began to flow down my face as he prayed for me. He then asked me if I wanted to be saved and give my life to God? I nodded through the tears, and as he prayed for me, the Holy Spirit began to come upon me, and I could no longer control what I was saying. I remember hearing some of the mothers of the church say, "That's the Holy Ghost, baby. Be glad about it!" What an experience. What a first introduction.

Now, here's the part of the story that I want to focus on for just a moment. I heard the mothers tell me, "That's the Holy Spirit." Even though I absolutely knew that I was having some sort of amazing experience, some sort of amazing introduction to God, if you will, I still didn't know exactly who God was. It would not be until many years later in my life that I could firmly answer the same question that Simon Peter answered when Jesus asked, "Who do you say that I am?"

What about you? As you are reflecting upon your first introduction to God, did your first meeting take place as he delivered you from something, or maybe when he healed your body or protected you from danger? Maybe he spared your life in a car accident. Maybe you can remember going through the loss of a loved one, and you didn't know how you were going to get out of the bed each day? What about being in a relationship that ended in divorce? What are some of your life situations that began cultivating your answer of who God is? God has to ask the question because life is going to happen to all of us, and as life is happening, we need to be certain that we really know who God is. Sometimes life will take us through such a devastating storm that we feel like we won't make it through to the other side. We feel as if this particular storm was designed to take us out. But it's during those times that your answer to the question, "_____, who do you say that I am?" will firmly anchor you.

> Simon Peter answered, "You are the Messiah, the son of the living God." Jesus replied, blessed are you Simon son of Jonah, for this was not revealed to you by flesh and blood, but by my father in heaven." (Matt. 16:16–17, NIV)

Our answer to this very same question today is revealed the exact same way. The father in heaven reveals himself to us through each of our life events. Our relationship with God the father in heaven strengthens through each struggle that we have, each breath we take, each story that is created, and each question that is asked and answered in our interviews. Eventually, we find ourselves starting to stand just as strong as Simon Peter and declare without a doubt who God is.

But it doesn't stop there with just having a firm answer to who God is. (If you follow the rest of that passage in verses 18 and 19, Jesus then speaks purpose into Simon Peter's life and makes him an incredible promise.) Promises that are power packed! He tells him that even hell won't be able to overcome his purpose, and the authority that he now has on earth will be backed up in heaven. Think about it, that's some kind of contract. But guess what, we each have that same type of contract with God. When we know the answer to who God is, it begins to lead us to our own purpose and our own promises, just as it did for Simon Peter. Being able to firmly answer the question, *Who do you say I am?* during our interview with God helps us to land an amazing contract. A contract full of benefits, promises, and a generous compensation plan that is signed, sealed, and delivered by God.

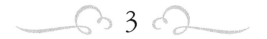

Who Do You Say I Am?

I believe that after we've answered the first question in our interview, then the next question is generally, *Who do you say I am?* Yes, I know that we just asked that question, but it's not a typo. This time it's our turn to ask God, "Who do you say I am, God?"

Think back for a moment. After Simon Peter answered the question of who Jesus was, then Jesus turned around and told him not only who he was, but also what his purpose was on this earth. Now, it's our turn to explore this answer with God to this question. It's our turn to ask God, "Who am I? God, I want to ask you the same question that you asked me: *who do you say I am?*"

I believe that God's response will not surprise each of us at all. Not really. Down inside of each of us are places that only God can touch. These places I call silos. By definition, a silo is a very deep underground chamber used for storage, or it can also be defined as "to isolate from others" (Google definitions, 2016). At times we allow circumstances and our emotional center to block us from responding from these deep places. We act as if our silos are off-limits to God. Have you ever heard of a silo mentality? It's a term that companies will sometimes use when one of their teams, departments, or organizations doesn't want to share their knowledge or ideas with their other departments or team members. Having a silo mentality inside of an organization or company can cause real problems because the connection to the overall structure and team mission is lost. A lot of times when there's a severe silo mentality, the result is a struggling company. These companies will usually have stunted or interrupted growth. These companies are literally killing themselves from the inside out. The same applies to us. When we deem our silos off-limits to God, we end up disconnected and feeling empty deep to our core.

Who did God create us to be in this world? We have to make sure that we don't have a silo mentality when it comes to hearing God's wisdom and his omniscience as to who we really are. God wants our heart-to-heart interviews to be conducted as a sharing process, not just a one-sided interview. He wants us to share with him our personal ideas as to who we feel that we were created to be in this world. He wants to hear the joy and the gratitude that we feel about the many gifts and talents that he has given us. He likes hearing us share how we are using those gifts to become the person that he created us to be before the very foundation of the world. But I also believe that he wants us to be very honest about whether or not who we are becoming in this world is congruent with his word. For example, sometimes we allow who we think that we are supposed to become to be shaped by what our friends, coworkers, and even parents have called us, instead of what God has spoken to us. And sometimes, what they have been calling us might absolutely be nothing close to who we were designed by God to be.

One of my favorite stories in the Bible is the story of Jacob. So much so that I seriously thought about naming my oldest son Jacob. I love the name and the story "Jacob the Supplanter." Imagine having twins, and one of them comes out of the birth canal holding on to the other one's foot. How could you name that child anything other than Jacob the supplanter? He came out of the womb trying to trip up or take Esau's place. And eventually, with a little help from his mother, he did just that. He took Esau's birthright. He became who he had been called from birth. Jacob acted, responded, and behaved exactly as he had been called. But the funny thing was that when the fulfillment of getting his brother's birthright came to fruition, Jacob was still not at rest. And he wasn't at rest partly because he allowed others to help define who he was instead of God.

Let's look at Jacob's name from just a slightly different perspective. Most names and words have multiple definitions. So what would Jacob's destiny have looked like if he had asked God to teach him how God himself defined *supplanter*? What if Jacob had said, "Why is this name a part of me? It doesn't seem as if it's a good thing to be called. But Lord, I know that you create only good things. So show me how to actually walk in my own birthright…After all, I am Abraham's grandson."

Think about it, what if Jacob had not had a silo mentality, but instead sought after God's wisdom to learn who he was created to be?

Another definition of *supplanter* is "to overthrow." I bet that we could all come up with many perspectives that could help someone "to thrive" if they saw themselves as the one who will overthrow. Perhaps that definition could have been viewed as someone who takes down evil. Being someone that will overthrow could have had the connotation that Jacob, you'll fight injustices to bring down corrupt governments; or maybe Jacob, you will lead military units to defeat your families' enemies. Imagine the difference if we allowed God to define our names.

So I told you that I loved the story of Jacob, and here's why. To me, Jacob is a story about a man who didn't realize that he was living his life in the shadows. He had the "not good enough" syndrome. He honestly thought that if he could have Esau's birthright, then he would become "good enough." So what do you do when the thing that you most wanted, you yearned for, you plotted for, you sweated for finally happens, but only for you to realize that it's about to take your life? That's what happened with Jacob. He finally had what he and his mother always dreamed that he would have in life, but he still wasn't fulfilled. Even worse, he was now in danger and had to run for his life.

We must not allow ourselves to be placed in danger like Jacob because we haven't sat through the interview process to find out who God says that we are. We have to allow God entrance into our deep empty silos and learn the answer to the question, God, who do you say I am? He will answer just as he did with Jacob.

As the story of Jacob continues, we learn that Jacob finally gets tired of running and living in fear. He is in a private place and finds himself wrestling with a man. (A lot of commentators say that this man was actually a form of God). Jacob then declares to the man, "I will not let you go until you Bless ME!" (Gen. 32:22–26, NIV). Jacob finally gets it. He wants what really belongs to him! "I want my birthright! I want what you, Oh God, have for me. I don't want my brother's life and his stuff. I want to be who you created me to be and to have what you want me to have for my life."

What an incredible story of a man finally coming to himself and submitting to becoming exactly who God ordained and created him to be.

After they wrestled all night long, God blesses Jacob and changes his name to Israel: "Triumphant with God or One who prevails with

God" (Gen. 27–31, NIV). Incredible, isn't it, that this supplanter, one who "overthrows," would be an example of how we too must overthrow (defeat) our false internal messages. You know those messages. Messages from fear that tell us that we are "not good enough," or those messages that are first cousins to those overpowering feelings that we are somehow inept or inadequate. We have to overthrow those messages so that we can possess our true birthright. Esau's birthright couldn't even compare to what God had in store for Jacob. Out of Jacob birthed the twelve tribes of Israel! Israel, God's chosen people. Israel, the nation that God spoke to and said, "You shall be my people and I shall be your God" (Jer. 30:22, NIV).

Stop settling and fighting for an Esau birthright;
Ask God; "Who do you say I am?"

4
What Did He Say?

When my youngest son was in preschool, we would pray out loud together every day on our car ride to school. We had this prayer time faithfully. Then one day after about a year of doing this, I guess he may have been about three years old, he said to me as I finished the prayer, "What did he say?"

I looked in the rear mirror and said, "Huh?"

He said to me again, "What did he say?"

I looked at him bewildered. I said, "What did who say? What are you talking about?"

My son replied, "Never mind, you didn't hear him."

Pretty profound for a three-year-old, wouldn't you say? And it was at that moment that I was reminded of the importance of having real conversations with God and not just operating in ceremonial habits.

You remember the Pharisees and the Sadducees? They were those religious, tradition, letter-to-the-law–speaking folks. Well, that day on that ride to school, I realized that I had sometimes been operating as a part of the Pharisee or Sadducee party unaware.

Those four little words, "What did he say?", totally changed how I began to view my conversations with God. It began to change how I responded to my interview calls with God. After that day, I began to seek to hear God's voice, even in the briefest moments of prayer. I began to want to not only hear his voice, but also have clarity and full understanding of his words.

Have you ever said good morning to someone, and they didn't say it back, or they murmured, and you couldn't understand what they were saying? Maybe they even spoke a different language, and you heard it loud and clear, but you still didn't understand what they were saying to you? That's how my conversations with God had been most days up until this point. Some days when I prayed, I would feel as if God wasn't saying anything back to me. I'd feel as if I wasn't getting a "Good morning" back from him. I called those prayers the "Job prayers." Other days, I would feel as if I could hear God's voice, but it was so faint that I didn't know exactly what he was saying to me—the "be still and patiently wait" prayers. Then there was the third type of conversation that I was having with God. I'd say, "Good morning, God." He'd reply loud and clear, "Buenos dias" or "Bonum mane."

Really, God? Really, that's what you are going to say back to me? I could hear him loud and clear, but what does that mean? I call those the "prophetic or transfigured" prayers. Prophetic or transfigured because that's usually when God tells you that something is going to come to pass in your life so amazing or so unbelievable that you can hardly wrap your mind around it. You don't have a clue how that thing is ever going to come to pass in your life, so the realm of it happening seems basically foreign to you. I bet that is how Abraham felt when God told him, "Abraham, you and Sara are going to have a child in your old age" (Gen. 17:15–17, NIV).

So what do you do when the interview with God is one-sided, not clearly heard, or seems foreign to you? I began to think about the story of Samuel for an answer to this question. In the story of Samuel, sometime after his mother gives him to the priest Eli in order to honor her promise to God, Samuel begins to start hearing his name being called by God. The passages tell us that Samuel awakes from his sleep and goes to the prophet Eli and says, "Here I am, you called me." Eli responds, "My son, I did not call; go back and lie down" (1 Sam. 3:4–5, NIV).

This dialogue between God and Samuel happened a total of three times before Eli realized that it was the Lord calling Samuel.

But Samuel didn't recognize the Lord's voice. Isn't it interesting that although Samuel had been in the temple learning about God, praying to God, and yes, assuredly chosen by God, that he still did not recognize God's voice? I can definitely relate to this uncertainty. There have been many times when I've questioned, "Was that you, Lord, speaking?"

Over the years, I've learned that the answer to being able to recognize God's voice requires at least two main components. The first requirement is setting the atmosphere for the presence of God to abide in, and second, making sure that we give our own personal response inside that same atmosphere that has been set. When Samuel lay in the temple where the ark of God was, he began to hear God, but the recognition of God's voice didn't come until Samuel responded with a spirit of readiness to receive what it was that God had in store for him. When we want to hear what God is saying clearly for our lives, we can set the atmosphere through fasting, reading his Word, devotion, worship, music, etc. Then all that we have to do is enter into his presence with a willing heart and a listening ear; ready to respond to his call.

In the previous chapter during our interview with God, we asked him, *"Who do you say I am?"* Now, I'm asking you, *"What did he say?"* It's time to clearly hear that answer. "Speak, Lord, for your servant is listening" (1 Sam. 3:9, NIV).

5
Why Am I Afraid?

During this interview process with God, I pray that if you don't already know his voice assuredly, that you will learn to recognize his voice. And if you do already recognize his voice in your life, then you will do as Eli and teach others. Knowing and hearing God's voice helps the storms in our lives to calm and the fear that can sometimes paralyze us to dissipate. So why at times are we still afraid?

As a clinical therapist, I found it interesting that there are more people diagnosed with anxiety disorders than any other mental disorder. I always thought that depression was the biggest mental illness problem that we had to face. But turns out, it's anxiety. As I learned more about anxiety and the underlying root of the problem, I could definitely understand why we are a society plagued with so much angst. Since fear seems to be at the very root of most of the anxieties that we face in life, it makes sense that this is the most commonly diagnosed mental disorder.

There are a lot of fears that everyone faces day to day, and that doesn't mean that they have an anxiety disorder. But what about when those fears become extreme, causing interruptions or severely impairing our lives? We might actually have something called a phobia. There are numerous lists of phobias all across the Internet as well as those classified in our medical journals. The lists are literally endless when it comes to phobias. Some phobias you could probably relate to, and other ones you might think, *Come on, you have got to be kidding me.* Phobias can be anything from an extreme fear of spiders, heights, animals, or crowded spaces, to and extreme fear of food, words, buttons, and more. The number of defined phobias goes well beyond what we can count because new ones are ever emerging as our world is ever changing.

But for now during this interview process, the question that has been asked is, why am I afraid? In this interview, you'll find that sharing with God those things that we are afraid of will ultimately begin to free us and position us into becoming who he has designed for us to be all along. In order for me to start living the life that God ordained for me to live, I had to allow him to heal me from my own personal phobia.

For many years, I personally suffered from thanatophobia. Doesn't sound pretty, does it? Well, it's not, and I began suffering from it as a teenager. And worst of all, I didn't even realize that I was suffering from this phobia. Thanatophobia means "fear of death." So how does a teenager start to fear death? When you are young, you are supposed to be fearless, throw caution to the wind, live and soak up life, right? So why was this not the case for me? There were really a number of factors that led me to having a fear of death. It would be too time-consuming to connect all the dots right now that led to this fear. However, the biggest factor that I'll contribute this fear to is when I lost my father.

When you lose a loved one, life changes. Life changes forever for you. And as a nineteen-year-old with one foot stepping out of childhood and the other trying to land into adulthood, it defined me. I'll never forget the day that my father passed away, even though on that day, it seemed as if the world literally stopped moving.

I was away in college. I was a sophomore, and on that exact day of his death, I was preparing to come home for the Easter holiday break. All that would be left for that semester was to return after break for final exams. My roommate was even coming home with me for the Easter break, and my best friend was going to drive the three of us home.

As we were preparing to leave, just minutes from getting on the road home, I received a phone call on the dorm hall phone from my grandmother (We didn't have cell phones then. LOL). My grandmother's words were very simple and direct. She just simply said,

"I need you to know that your father has passed. Come on home. Everything is going to be okay."

Honestly, I don't remember anything else that she may have said after those initial words. I just kind of remember standing there holding the phone, in shock, thinking that this is not real! How could this be real? Up until last month, he was walking around fine. Sure, he had had a surgery a few weeks ago, but he was going to recover, wasn't he? How could this possibly be real? And for me, it wasn't. It wasn't fully real.

I actually continued in that vein of thought for months, maybe even a year or more. No one knew that my world had been decimated. One week later, right after the funeral and Easter break, I returned back to school. I finished my finals with all As, and I even began a very challenging summer school session that June. During that summer session, I was required to take gross anatomy. This was my most challenging class. It was challenging not because of the information that I had to learn, but because it required cutting on a human corpse every day. And I guess if that wasn't enough to challenge me, my assigned cadaver was a forty-five-year old African American man that had died from cancer, same as my father. But guess what, I tightened up my mask that I was hiding behind, and I kept moving. My mask was great. It was full of confidence, strength, and courage. And best of all, it was completely stoic; nothing got in, and nothing got out emotionally.

That summer, I continued to work hard every day to learn every single nerve and muscle in the human body. By now, you might be wondering why would I do all this? Why would I put myself through working on a dead body every day? Why didn't I just take a break from school? Didn't taking a break make more sense? Surely, that was too much too soon. Well, the real reason is simple as to why I didn't take a break. *I was afraid!* My universe had been completely altered, and I was afraid and confused as to how to live inside of it.

My secret was that at that point in my life, I was stuck. I was afraid to live. I was afraid to live life without my father, but I was also just as afraid of death. I was afraid of dying without completing school. I was afraid of dying and never marrying. I was afraid of dying and never having a family. I was afraid of so many things, and I wasn't even aware that fear had not only started to define me, but it also defined a lot of my life choices. It was that fear that blocked me for so many years from being who God said that I was to be. It was that fear that even at other times later in life, when I would dare to venture into pursuing who I was called to be, that would halt me and cripple me. It was that fear that would say to me go sit down somewhere. You don't want to chance interrupting your life again, do you? After all, isn't this an okay life? Isn't this a comfortable life? Sure it is. It's a safe life." Although I may have been stuck in life, it was that overwhelming *fear* that was my best-kept secret. It was its strong hold that kept me from fully walking into who God was calling me to be.

I wish that I could tell you that the fear was easily broken. I wish that I could tell you that one day God instantly delivered me and gave me a miracle that broke all my chains. But the truth is that God allowed me to face new challenges over the years, and I allowed those challenges to intensify my fear. As the old adage says, "What do you do when your biggest fear becomes your reality?" Well, for me, the fear of that reality lay in the fact that I was my father's child.

People would often tell me, "You look so much like your father. You even have his mannerisms." And I did. I have so many of his traits, even down to his handwriting, and it scared me beyond comprehension. I am my father's child! I would ruminate as to whether my same fate would be as his, dying by forty-five? I would wonder when death would show up at my house again. Would I live to see my children grow up? I'd think over and over about death, and my thanatophobia haunted me.

So now imagine how that fear must have intensified when I was diagnosed at the age of thirty-seven with a rare cancer. Imagine how those words that everyone spoke regarding my resemblance to my father impacted my life. Imagine how those continuous words, although meant to compliment me, just fed my fear of death. It wasn't their fault; they didn't know that I had been diagnosed with one of the rarest cancers that a person could have. They didn't know that they were nurturing my thanatophobia with each comparison made between me and my father. And I didn't dare share that reality with anyone. I was becoming less and less like the person who God had designed me to be because the fear was slowly drifting me down a different course, an unintended course for my life. A course without many rifts and waves. It was an easy-to-navigate, safe course, but don't mistake it; it was still the wrong course for the call that was on my life.

I would pretend that I was in the game of life, but I was really just existing behind a firmly worn mask, praying that I wasn't going to die young. During one of my many interviews with God, he asked me, "Why are you so afraid?" And I finally gave him the real answer. It was not as if he didn't already know, but he was waiting on me to openly and freely share with him so that he could then teach me how to be released from the fear, so that it could no longer control or block my destiny.

I believe that this question is one of the greatest questions to dialogue with God in your heart-to-heart interview. Make sure that you are really present as you are answering this question with him. It may be a hard question to answer, but in order for you to accept the next position that God has for your life, it is critical that you fully answer, *Why am I afraid?*

6

How Do I Break the Fear?

I once heard that there are 365 times in the Bible where it says, "Fear not." And that's because God knew that we would need a dose of courage daily. That courage is definitely needed when you are called by God to fulfill a purpose. When we begin hearing and understanding who God says we are, we may experience a myriad of emotions. Sometimes it will be excitement and exhilaration that we feel. Other times it may be fear, overwhelm, and confusion. During those times that we feel excitement and exhilaration, it's as if everything has finally come into focus, and we now *know* exactly who we were meant to be in Christ. But usually before we can even get started moving forward toward our destiny, the other set of emotions start knocking at the door: good old fear and his cousins, confusion and overwhelm, who are boldly walking hand in hand with a load of their buddy, self-doubt. When those cousins visit, we may start to back up a little and ask God, "Why me, God? Did I really just hear you say that? Did I really just hear you say that I'm supposed to build this, become that, go there, do that? Did I really just hear you say that?"

"I'm not equipped, Lord." Does any of this sound familiar? If so, that's when we really need to just take a little pause and let God do the talking. Let him lead the interview. At this point, let him remind you of his résumé and his leadership skills. Let him remind you how he told Noah to go build an *ark* to protect his family from a flood, when there had never even been rain before on the earth. Let him remind you how he told Abraham to kill his promised son, Isaac, and then provided the ram in the bush. Let him tell you how he told Moses to lead the children of Israel free from Pharaoh's hand, the same Pharaoh whose family had raised Moses and took care of him as their own son.

After reflecting upon God's résumé a little more, it might just remind us that it doesn't matter what family or class that we come from in life. But what matters is that when we sit for our interview, the interview that will ultimately lead us to purpose and destiny, we are willing to accept the position when it's offered. Isn't this exciting? God is getting ready to offer you your next position!

Have you ever been offered a job right there on the spot and then turned it down, or turned to the interviewer and said, "Are you sure that you want to hire me?" Imagine hearing God say, "I want you. I want you for the purpose of __[fill in the blank]__." And you answer, "No, I don't think that I can accept that position, God." How would that sound? I imagine God would just shake his head and tell Gabriel, "Hey, we got another Jonah here."

Don't get me wrong. I understand that we are only human, and that it is natural for walls of fear to creep in as well as self-doubt, whispering to us messages of inadequacy sometimes when God offers us certain positions. But breaking those fears doesn't have to seem so impossible. We just need to remember the fact that God offers on-the-job training. Whom he calls, he will equip.

God gave Noah a very elaborate blueprint for the ark. I don't even know if Noah was a trained carpenter, but he was hired. Not only that, it took Noah somewhere between 70–120+ years to complete the project. (Theologians still debate the exact number of years. But either way, he had to have received some extensive on-the-job training.) And either way, Noah developed into a master craftsman. It was Noah's acceptance of an incredible position that led to an unparalleled purpose: the purpose of helping to replenish the earth.

Those walls of fear that have been built in our lives can be broken. It may be a long and tedious process, but the walls can come down. When we realize that it is those walls of fear that have been preventing us from the full benefit package that God offers, such benefits as peace that passes all understanding, joy full of strength and glory, love that's inexplicable, and so much more. When we come to this realization, we'll find ourselves starting to do everything that we possibly can to break through those walls.

Have you ever seen the movie *The Shawshank Redemption*? In the movie, there's a part of the story line where the inmate, played by Morgan Freeman, is so focused on breaking through his prison walls that every night, he takes time to use a fork and scrape a little mortar off the wall. Can you imagine the futility that he must have felt each night when he began that process? Can you imagine what others would have said if he had shared with them what he was doing to that wall each night? But he had a determination to break through that wall. So he continued to scrape away at it daily. It may have taken him years, but eventually, he created a large-enough break in the wall that he was able to tunnel all the way through to the other side. And that's what happens when we become truly determined to break down those mountainous walls of fear. We'll do whatever it takes to break free and get to the other side. Our fears will begin to break more and more as we understand deep down in our spirit and soul that God has called us for purpose, and that purpose can literally change the world. Our part is to sit for the interviews, accept the positions when offered, and then show up daily, willing to work hard. It is this simple process that somehow manages to shape us into who we were always meant to become in life. It is this process that positions us for our call to purpose.

There is tremendous freedom on the other side of that wall of fear, and it's not just our freedom. Someone else is in need of us having the ability and stick-to-it-iveness to tear down that wall. Someone else is in need of us boldly accepting the position that God has offered. Someone else needs what's inside of us, so that they too can begin to move forward and live freely. For Noah, it was an entire nation of people who depended upon him accepting his purpose! So *how do we break the fear?* First, start by accepting the position that God is offering.

7

What's Next?

Now that we are tunneling through the walls of fear, and they are beginning to crumble, what's next? I believe that the answer to this question is different for each one of us. And I also believe that because this answer does vary for each of us that it becomes highly critical that we become intentional about taking notes during or immediately after each of our interviews with God.

I have had interviews with God where he wakes me up at three or four o'clock in the morning. I'm sure that you have had those kinds too. "Why, God? Why do you want to talk so early? Can't we talk at 8:00 a.m. or so in the morning, after I've had my coffee?" LOL.

But seriously, here's what I've learned. I've learned to always take good notes during my interviews or immediately afterward so that I don't lose critical information. Most of us call that journaling. When journaling, write down the questions that God is asking so that later you can do research; write down the feelings that you are experiencing so that you can praise him during each step of the way. And most importantly, write down the position that he is offering so that the vision can begin to be made plain.

For me, God told me at a very young age one of the main positions that he had for my life. And even though I clearly heard the position and I did accept it, the on-the-job training has not only been continuous for many years, but it has also been very challenging. Also, it definitely hasn't been a straight line for me as I learned how to walk into that position, or maybe I should say that call on my life. There have been many bumps and detours, and I even used to say derailments. You know those kinds of derailments when you feel as if the very foundation of your soul has been shaken, and you wonder is it even worth the fight to get back up and back on track again?

What I've learned from those derailments is that most of the time, they were not really derailments at all. They were either fears trying to creep back in, or they were really *train stops*. More specifically in my case, they were actually *trip stops* and *fixed train stops*. When I thought that the entire train had flipped off the rails and sometimes even turned over, in actuality, it was a "trip stop" or "a fixed train stop" being activated by God. It felt like derailment, but now I know that it really wasn't at all. Imagine being on a fast-moving train that missed all the stops. How scary would that be? We'd call that a runaway train, and we'd have to get others involved to slow that train down so that we could bring it to a stop and hopefully get it on the right path again.

That's exactly how I had gotten at one point in my life. I was going through life so fast that I was missing most of the signals. I wasn't really listening anymore during my interviews with God. Not really. But I was telling myself that I was totally tuned in to him. But in actuality, I had everything all mapped out my way. And I started mapping things out because I had heard him offer a couple of assignments and given me one or two pieces of the puzzle.

I was so in charge that I was blowing right past those train stops. Train stops where I was supposed to let people out of my life because they were only placed there for a season. Train stops where I was supposed to drop off jobs, but I didn't want to give up that financial comfort and false security. But most of all, imagine blowing right past the train stops where I was supposed to put off church tradition, but I missed it because I didn't even know that it was a passenger. I was missing every one of those stops. I was a fast-moving runaway train.

So what happened next? Well, because God loves me so much, he had to activate the *trip stop*. "A trip stop is part of a railway signaling system that serves as a train protection device designed to automatically stop a train if it attempts to pass a signal when the operating rules prohibit such movement, or in other applications if the train attempts to pass at an excessive speed" (Wikipedia, 2011).

God had been trying to get me to slow down and see the red signals, but I refused to see them because not only was my hearing impaired, but my vision had been compromised. I had stopped writing the vision and letting him order my steps. I had tons of journals, but they hadn't been written in for years. I had tons of goals, but when I did bother to write them down, I hardly ever revisited them. The true vision behind the position that God had offered to me so many years ago had been lost. And a big part of the reason why it was lost was because I had stopped writing, reading, and growing by his vision.

I was a runaway train caught up in the cares of life. Let me put it like this: I was caught up in the busy cycles of earning a living, social media, soccer mom, and more. I didn't realize that I was a runaway because I kept telling myself that it was good that I was busy and being pretty productive. After all, I was living a clean life, and I was helping people in the process. So what in the world is wrong with that? Well, the missing element was that I wasn't *becoming*. I wasn't becoming who God had specifically designed for me to be inside of the position that he had offered to me. There was nothing wrong with the things that I was doing. But that was the critical point that I wasn't grasping. I was *doing* instead of *becoming*!

I was moving so fast that even the *trip stop* didn't stop me. I just soared right past the device. So what happens next when even the trip stop doesn't stop you from passing the red signals like it was designed to do? Well, God, in his infinite mercy, then provided the *fixed train stop*. This type of train stop stops the train from moving too fast. And that's exactly what I needed to do. I needed to stop moving so fast. In other words, I needed to stop being so busy. I had to stop being so busy in life and church. See, you can be busy in church for all the wrong reasons. So I needed to get back to where my life was centered around the right priority, and that priority was being busy about my father's business.

Now, for just a moment, I want you to think about an Amtrak train moving at a speed of over 100 mph, and then having to immediately come to a complete stop in a very short period of time. Think about it, what if you weren't aware that the train was about to stop? What if you weren't aware that things were about to become completely still? What if you weren't aware that a trip stop or a fixed train stop even existed? You'd probably become terrified! You'd probably think, *Oh my god, the train just derailed! Am I still alive?* I'd bet to a degree, you'd feel just like I did. And that is that total disaster had occurred. My over-100-mph-moving train had just come to an absolute complete halt, and I had no idea that the stop was coming.

Initially, when that fixed train stop was activated, I didn't even begin to comprehend that my train was still on the track and that it actually didn't flip over nor had it derailed after all. So since I didn't understand this, I began looking to sort through the perceived rubble of my life. You know the kind of rubble. The rubble that was my lost job because my department had closed, the rubble of no longer having friends and family as emotional and physical support in a close proximity because we had just moved to a different state, and even the rubble of having to learn a new way to experience God because I was no longer a part of the church that I had grown up in from childhood to adulthood. No, initially, I absolutely did not understand that God had activated a fixed train stop and not a derailment. And it definitely didn't feel as though he activated the fixed train stop out of love and for my own protection.

Once I finally realized that my train had not derailed off the tracks and that instead I was actually being protected, I realized that I was actually being given another chance to let God correct my compromised hearing and vision and to start writing his vision for my life plainly again. I was being given an amazing second chance to move forward through God's lenses and plans for my life. And as I began to diligently search God for the answers to what was next for my life, I learned to not leave out the all-important *how* when talking to God. "How do you want me to do things, God?" "How do you want to order my steps?" But what was most interesting was that when I started seeking how God wanted to order things in my life, I ultimately developed a new type of relationship with him. I got a chance to know God in an entirely new way. I began experiencing how to sit for interviews with God, my friend.

At some point in our lives, the interviews will shift from a conversation with our boss, who is indeed the ultimate creator, the giver of all life, the Great I am that I am, to having conversations with our closest friend. A friend who is excited to see us; a friend who has done that, been there, and got that T-shirt; a friend who eagerly awaits to help us; a friend who will activate those trip stops or fixed train stops when needed; but most of all, a friend who loves us unconditionally and is willing to share the secret of *what's next* for our lives.

8

What Are You Willing to Share?

When a great friendship develops, you begin to share things with one another without even thinking about it. I've had friendships over the years that had become so close that not only did we share such things as secrets, food, clothes, and more, but we also eventually started to share living space. We moved in together.

As a result of living with a couple of my close friends, I learned some important life lessons. Fortunately for me, most of those lessons were pretty beneficial. Notice that I use the word *beneficial* and not *good*. In life, a lot of experiences that occur may not seem good, they may not feel good, and they sure don't look good at the time, but if you allow the experiences to become life lessons, they can turn into benefits.

> And we know that in all things God works for the good of those who love him, who have been called according to his purpose. (Rom. 8:28, NIV)

There were so many of those *in all things* that didn't seem good at the time, but still managed somehow to become beneficial for me and my family later in life. It's those *in all things* that sometimes still have us scratching our heads, trying to examine how did that just work out in our favor. How did I already know how to handle this situation? How did I instinctively know what to do and what to say next? And it will also be those experiences that happened years ago in your life that didn't seem good at the time, but are now placing you before presidents, CEOs, clergy, and providing you with enormous benefits.

Believe it or not, as a teenager, I used to get in fights occasionally. Even though I knew that this was wrong. I would never start a fight, but I sure wouldn't back away from any. I was very assertive, and I loved a good challenge, even if it was a physical one. So my mind-set was "bring it on!"

One day, when I was about sixteen, one of my very good friends and I had a misunderstanding that led to what I call a heated fellowship. And before I knew it, she had slapped me firmly across the face. I was in total shock because I had been friends with this person from a very young age, and we had experienced many heated fellowships, but never, not once, had either of us ever laid hands on one another.

My first thought of course was to hit her back, but for a split second, I decided to pause and think before I responded. Up until that point, I had always reacted to situations, and I didn't understand that there was a difference between reacting and responding. Even though my mother would often tell me, "Stephanie, stop letting how people act cause you to react." I tell you, if I had a quarter for every time that she told me that, I'd be a wealthy woman.

So many things went through my mind in that split second of processing. I thought, *I can't fight in this house, that's disrespectful to my friend's parents. If I get into a fight here, my parents are going to ground me for life. If I fight her, I'm probably going to have to fight her siblings as well. How am I going to get back home if I fight back?* (I didn't drive that day. LOL.) As you can see, a lot of things went through my mind in that short period of time. And that's when I decided to do something that I wasn't accustomed to doing. I decided to respond. I decided to analyze things and make a conscious choice instead of a reactive emotional one. And the choice that I made that day was not to strike back. This may seem like a small thing to do, but for me as a sixteen-year-old at that time, this was a huge feat for me. It was a life lesson that would blossom into a strong virtue and dominant part of a skill set that would become essential for my life. In the end, my friend and I sorted things out and cleared up the misunderstanding. She apologized to me that day, and to this day, some twenty years later, we remain very good friends.

Sometimes, I look back on that single experience as the day that I started maturing enough to demonstrate temperance. It was that experience that began to build the muscle of temperance, and it is that temperance that has literally saved my life on several occasions. The benefits of learning to respond instead of react began for me with what didn't feel like a good experience at the time, but somehow became one of those *in all things* experiences that later works for your good. Thankfully, this experience began to cultivate the temperance that I would need to draw from over and over in my life.

For instance, some three years later, I found myself having to help diffuse someone else's argument. This time it could have been much more than a fistfight. It could have been life or death. On that day, I was literally just walking into a building, when all of a sudden, these two ladies began arguing quite loudly. It became a heated fellowship very quickly, and a gun was drawn before I could even take another step. I was trapped right in the middle. But it was temperance that allowed me to speak peace long enough for security to come. It was temperance that probably saved my life and maybe one of theirs that day.

Over the years, temperance has become one of my best gifts. I have had to draw from her on numerous occasions, and I thank God for revealing the benefits of her fruit to me. When I began work as a new clinical therapist, I had a lot of duties because our department staff was so small. So if someone was off from work for a vacation day or a sick day, then you were the only one working that day. Well, one day early on in my new position, I found myself as the only one on duty that day, and wouldn't you know it, I had to draw from temperance again to help preserve my life.

One of the clinic's long-time patients came in demanding to be seen by his regular therapist, and when I explained that she was not working on that day, he became very agitated. So agitated that he became violent, and he later pulled a knife. So how do you stay steady and not react but instead respond when a six-feet-plus burly man corners you alone in a small clinic? Oh, and did I mention that at the time he was also psychotic? At that time he was having active auditory hallucinations. For me, I simply responded by having a quick interview with my friend, God the father, and he speedily ordered my lips as to what to say in order to diffuse the situation just as quickly as it had occurred.

Some may think that when you work in a psychiatric setting that this is just a skill set that you have to learn in order to be a good therapist. But I believe that it is more than that. I believe that temperance is good fruit that my friend in heaven continued to share with me over and over so as to help cover and protect me during one of my most satisfying life positions. Over the years, I have had several other potentially dangerous, maybe even life-threatening situations to occur at work. As I reflect back upon each of them, I am sure now that God was using those *in all things* way back as that immature sixteen-year-old to begin molding me for the position of therapist.

As we continue our interview with God our friend, I believe that he will continue to share so many benefits. His benefit package is like no other. Some benefits you'll recognize right off as being good for your life. Other benefits may begin as those *in all things* before they reveal themselves unto you as working for your good. But one thing that I want you to rest assuredly in is this: when we get to know God as a true friend, the one who is closer than any brother, then we become extremely grateful to be able to share our secrets, our time, and most importantly our living space with him. Real friends love sharing with one another. They just can't help themselves. If I had not allowed God to reside with me, live inside of me, I don't know if my friend would have been able to share as much good fruit with me as he has over the years. His fruit has helped to spare my life. His fruit has worked for the good in so many cases for my life.

I challenge you to take a moment and reflect upon some of the things that God, your friend, has shared with you over the years. And then answer back, *what am I willing to share?*

9

How Have You Changed?

One of my absolute favorite quotes is by Gandhi: "You must become the change you wish to see in the world." Many times we can get lost in complaining about what is not right in our lives. We begin to become like a scratched record that plays the same lyrics over and over again. Lyrics that sound something like this: My job is a dead end. It is just not satisfying. My children are all over the place. My spouse is working my nerves. Ever found yourself saying some of these things?

These might be some of the things that we are tempted to say when our closest friend is conducting the interview. I once had to interview a good friend for a position, and it was not at all what I expected. I thought that since we were such close friends, she would bring her A game into the interview and share all the great qualities that she possessed. But instead, she did the exact opposite.

Now imagine, would you sit across from God, who is your closest friend and who has been gracious enough to interview you for a higher position, and then proceed to tell him all the things that you feel are wrong with the position that he's offering? How would it sound telling God, "I know that you are the creator, but these children that you gave me, God, are off the chain. You need to fix them." Or "I can't believe that you allowed this to happen in my marriage. " "God, I think that this position was not the one that you really intended for me."

Think about it, that is exactly what we sometimes do in our prayer interviews. We bring God a laundry list of complaints. We bring God our laundry list of the things that we feel are not right instead of asking him to equip us and change us to be better for the position. And the most interesting thing is that while we are presenting these complaints during our interview, we tend to forget that we were the ones that asked for the position. We prayed for those children and cried out many nights for God to send us our Boaz or Ruth.

Instead of complaining about what's not right with the position, I've learned to thank him for the position and pray that he'll show me how to become an agent of change. A lot of times we are placed in certain situations because God wants us to learn how to shine even in the strangest of places or circumstances. Instead of us complaining about our children, what are other avenues that we could take? Have you ever encountered someone who was just a natural-born mother? I mean motherhood just oozes out of them. They find extreme joy and fulfillment in being a mother. I have, and she gave birth to me.

My mother is the mother of all mothers, and you would think that since I came from her, then that would be my natural position too. But that is absolutely not the case. However, what I have learned to do over the years is to sit down with her and interview her. I ask her questions on effective parenting, and this has been an effective solution, seeking godly counsel from her and others who I know are also amazing parents. Instead of complaining, we can seek more resources and let God know at the same time that we are up for this assignment, and we are willing to work hard in our position.

We must be the agent of change. The only person that we can change in this world is the one who looks back at us in the mirror. But we can influence others by how we demonstrate love, concern, encouragement, and so much more. Instead of us complaining about our spouse, what if we started studying how to speak their love language fluently? I learned a few years back that my husband spoke a totally different love language than the one that I speak. So sometimes it was like living in a house where I spoke English, and he spoke Igbo. By the way, my husband really does speak Igbo as he's from Nigeria. So what do you do when you don't have a clue what the other person is saying? You spend time learning each other's native language. Is it challenging? It most definitely is. But it is also very fulfilling and rewarding. Even greater than the reward of learning to speak those love languages is the fact that it helps for the development of yet another of God's greatest positions, marriage.

Change is so critical in every position in life. I once heard a story of a good old man named Mr. Simpson who was as consistent as they get. Mr. Simpson was a man who worked in the same factory for over thirty years, doing the same job every day. That is a feat in itself, wouldn't you say? Day in and day out, Mr. Simpson would come to work, punch in on time, and perform his job without change or problem. Every day he fully did what was required. Mr. Simpson wasn't a very friendly man, but he also didn't bother anyone, and after all, being friendly wasn't part of the job requirement.

Then one day, as time and luck would have it, a lead management position became available at the factory. Mr. Simpson made up his mind to apply for that position. He along with everyone else who worked at the factory just knew that he was totally a shoo-in for the position. No one else had the kind of record that he possessed. His record was superb. So he applied for the position. He was absolutely sure that with all his experience, he would land the job.

A few days later, to Mr. Simpson's surprise, another worker who had only been at the factory for five years was offered the lead position. Mr. Simpson was irate! He couldn't believe that after all these years of hard work and dedication, he had been passed over for the promotion. He demanded to see the hiring supervisor, and he began to remind the supervisor as to how he had been with the company for over thirty years. How he worked every day unchanged, without fail, and without any problems with anyone. Mr. Simpson demanded to know how anyone could be more qualified than him. He demanded to know why he had been passed over for the position that should have been rightfully his position.

The supervisor simply said, "Well, Mr. Simpson you are right on a couple of things. You have worked for thirty years now unchanged, without fail, and without any problems with anyone. And to me, it would seem that that means that for those last twenty-nine years, you haven't learned anything new beyond your first year. Mr. Simpson, you haven't changed. You haven't changed, not one little bit."

Do we sometimes behave like Mr. Simpson? We show up for our positions, but we are really just going through the motions. Do we operate as agents of change in certain areas of our lives but not others because we are extremely comfortable? Reflect back on a few situations in your life that you know have absolutely caused you to grow. Would you trade those experiences? Would you trade what you've learned and the person that you have become because of those experiences?

Now take a moment and reflect on a few life experiences that you sat back, much like Mr. Simpson, and you refused to be stretched and developed by God. You refused to grow. Make a comparison between those situations that you decided to only survive versus those you made up your mind to thrive in. What are some of the differences? What are some things that you now know that could have made you an even greater agent of change?

I have a simple three-step formula that I ascribe to as it pertains to change in my life:

Step One: I seek to hear God.
Step Two: I make a point to serve others.
Step Three: I intentionally work on myself to grow.

Over the years, this simple process has helped me to grow, develop, and change during the different seasons in my life. Change can be a very scary process at times, but it is also one of the few constants of life. So we have to keep asking God to help us to embrace change, and then we have to be willing to share those stories of how we've changed. At my church, we call those stories testimonies, and we believe that we can become an overcomer by the power of the words of our testimonies. So don't hold back. Share with others *how have you changed.*

10

Why Am I Hurting?

When my oldest son was around eight years old, I took him to the doctor because he constantly complained of his legs hurting. The pain was sometimes so severe that it would wake him up during the night. I would put heating pads on his legs, anoint him, and massage his legs a little, but he still had pain. So finally, we went to the doctor for a checkup and diagnosis. I'll admit at that time, I was a little afraid as to what the doctor would tell me was wrong with my child because rheumatoid arthritis (RA) ran in my family. I myself had been diagnosed with juvenile RA at the age of thirteen, and the doctors had told my parents that my case would be so severe that I would be cripple, confined to a wheelchair by the time that I was eighteen. All that I will say about having been given that shocking diagnosis is that I thank God that my mother and father knew how to have great interviews with God. They also began teaching me from that day forward how to prepare and sit for my own interviews with God because they knew that at a very young age, God would begin calling me to interview for many positions throughout my life.

So when we arrived for my son's appointment, they conducted a normal history profile, and then they did a full lab workup. When his test results came back, they told me that everything was well with my son, and they believed that he just had *growing pains.* They went on to explain that it was very common for young children to experience these types of pains. They told me that my son was going to grow very tall and that he was also growing very fast, and this was not at all anything to worry about. They also went on to tell me that there was not much that I could do to help rid him of the pain, but in time, he'd naturally overcome it.

As we are going through our own process of change and answering the question posed in the last chapter, *how have I changed?*, we may have also found ourselves very keenly aware of the fact that even though we are changing and beginning to feel purpose and a sense of fulfillment, we are also experiencing at times some nagging and unrelenting pains in our life. So why are we hurting when we know that we are definitely moving forward in the right direction? Well, my friend, it's probably because you are experiencing *growing pains.*

God has so many companies. Too many to even begin to try to number. Some of his companies are Fortune 500 companies full of wealth, glam, and glitter, and we want to join those right away; while others may not seem as profitable, glamorous, or as rich, and we might think that we couldn't possibly be called for an interview with one of those type of mom-and-pop companies that he owns. But we have to remember that everything that God owns is exceptional and designed for purpose.

When we are experiencing those growing pains in our lives, I can think of two specific companies that we are probably earning stock in. God loves these two little companies. In these often undervalued and overlooked companies, he serves as the CEO, CIO, sometimes the entire executive board, and he creates and brands the most exquisite products. In these two little companies, God gets to get his hands dirty, and it is in these two little companies as you are acquiring your shares, you will also experience some of your greatest growing pains. These companies are his refinery companies and his potter's houses.

"Inside of an oil refinery, crude oil is processed and refined into more useful products like petroleum, gasoline, kerosene and more. These oils are then used for an array of purposes such as becoming light sources, heating sources, and even providing pharmaceutical needs just to name a few. However, the process of refining that crude oil into *purpose* doesn't come easy. Not only do those crude oils (the garbage and the baggage that we have in our lives) have to go through a process of reforming, isomerization—*defined as rearranging the atoms in a molecule so that the product has the same chemical formula but a different structure*—and more but the crude oil must also experience being processed under extreme temperatures. Those temperatures can range from 104ºF to greater than 1112ºF depending upon the use that it is being made into" (American Fuel & Petrochemical Manufacturers, 2015).

As God begins to refine us for his use, the heat begins to get turned way up in our lives. Things and even people sometime get broken loose from our lives. People that we thought would stay with us forever are transitioned to different geographical locations, different relationship statuses with us, and yes, sometimes they are even transitioned beyond this realm to their eternal home. Of course, that type of transition is the toughest to grow through. But it is during our growing pains, during our time of earning shares inside of God's refinery, that God is nearest to us.

It is during those times that even though it may seem as if we are in constant pain and it may feel as if we can barely speak because the refining process is so great, we learn the power and the joy of a whisper. In the refinery, the workers have to keep a close watch as the oils are being processed and refined. They have to make sure that the temperature doesn't exceed a certain limit so as to cause an explosion. So it is imperative that they keep a close watch. The same is true of God; as we are being refined for his purpose, we begin to learn that since he is the chief refiner, he can't help but to abide close by us and protect his exquisite creations. Because of the fact that he does abide so close to us during our refining process, there is not a need for us to have to cry loud or to scream and shout in order to get his attention. In the refinery, God is so near to us that all that we have to do is *whisper*, and he hears us. Just a soft whisper, and he sees about us!

> He said, "Look! I see four men walking around in the fire, unbound and unharmed, and the fourth looks like the Son of God." (Dan. 3:25, NIV)

Don't worry, even though you might be in pain and uncomfortable right now, those are just normal natural growing pains that you are experiencing, and we all eventually grow right out of them.

Days will come in your life where you may find yourself sitting back, analyzing and performing introspection over your life. Days where you will begin to reflect upon some of your previous interviews. Interviews where you felt certain that you were becoming exactly who God wanted you to be, but then you wondered why you were still feeling so much pain. So much pain that you began to ask yourself, *"Why am I hurting?"* Well, I want you to just remind yourself that you are just experiencing growing pains, and not only are you growing, but you are also earning some very lucrative stock in one of God's greatest refinery companies.

11

Who Is in Your Tribe?

When I was growing up, my parents would occasionally caution me to make sure that I'm being careful about who I am hanging out with and choosing as my circle of friends. They would say that friendships have a way of shaping who you become, so choose carefully. At the time, I didn't realize just how right they were about selecting friends. It wasn't until recently, after I found myself asking my oldest child some very similar questions to the ones that my parents had asked me about my friendships, that I understood the importance of your circle of friends.

I began to ask him, "What kind of values do your friends have? Are they good people? What sort of things do you and your friends talk about when you hang out? Are any of them Christians? Are any of them saved, born again, spirit filled?" I went on and on with questions. Finally, he looked at me, probably with the same look that I used to give my parents, and he simply replied, "Mom, I don't think about those things when I'm with my friends. They are just my friends. They are good people. So does all that other stuff really matter?" I thought to myself, *Son, one day you will understand just how much it matters.*

As adults, we begin to truly understand just how critical our relationships and friendships are to our well-being and purpose. We've probably all heard the saying that we are the average of the five people that are in our closest friendship circle. Once or twice over the years, I've actually taken a moment to examine my present tribe and see if that statement holds true? I'll examine whether or not my income is roughly the average of my tribe. Is my spiritual development roughly the average of my tribe? And is my family lifestyle roughly the average of my tribe? You may be wondering, how does someone decide the average of spiritual development and family lifestyle? Well, the way I look at it is like this: Does my tribe push me to grow or develop more in these areas of my life? Does my tribe encourage me to explore ways to spread the gospel? Does my tribe encourage me to branch out? And most defining to me is, does my tribe challenge me to stop reaching for low-hanging fruit?

I learned a long time ago that a very good way to build strength and courage is to be willing to climb those huge metaphorical trees that are present in our life and then venture the risk of going out on the limbs. A lot of times, out on those limbs is where we'll find some great fruit. Do the tree limbs break sometimes? Yes, unfortunately they do. But often times when those limbs break, God miraculously keeps us from getting seriously injured. And then he usually will teach us a different technique to use when making our climbs. Instead of us giving up after our falls, God shows us how to minimize the risks in order to get to the best fruit.

Since God doesn't ever want us to get seriously hurt, he may suggest different things to help us with the climb. Things like wearing a harness and perhaps having a spotter below so as to climb as if you are on a mountain. Sometimes he'll even show us a different tree to climb that has better fruit on it for us. The fruit on the tree that God is showing us may digest better in our lives. We have to make sure that we don't become too busy listening to others talk about the fruit that they got off the first tree, the same tree that we fell off numerous times, that we can't hear God when he's telling us to go somewhere else to climb. When he is saying, "This is your tree to climb, not that other one," God is our ultimate counsel, so we must make sure that we are listening closely with open hearts. He is still thoroughly enjoying our interviews, and he loves continuing the heart-to-heart matters of discussion with us, his dear friends.

Have you ever had an interviewer mix things up a little by deciding to bring in a second or even a third person to ask a few questions or to share a different perspective during an interview? I have. And at first, it can feel very intimidating. After we have fallen off that proverbial tree, I believe that God will sometimes bring others into our interviews. Not to intimidate us, but instead to encourage us and to provide a different perspective.

God will call for a second, maybe even a third or fourth party to come join our interview. It may be a friend, colleague, pastor, or sometimes even a perfect stranger who we meet in the store. But he makes sure to send someone into our interview. He sends someone who can confirm or encourage us to keep exploring. Someone who can encourage us to keep getting back up after the falls, someone to tell us to keep learning and applying what we've learned because one day it will eventually help us reach the best fruit. He sends someone into our interviews to encourage us to keep moving higher and not to dare even think about reaching for that low-hanging fruit again!

Our tribe is absolutely crucial! Having a tribe made up of like-minded individuals who share the same values is critical. Having a tribe of individuals who love having their own interviews with God and sharing their experiences from those heart-to-heart interviews can be life changing. But best of all, having a tribe of individuals who can hear God, give wise counsel, and be willing to sit in the toughest of interviews right next to you when needed is the greatest of all tribes. It is those kind of tribes that help us to grow and succeed in each of our climbs. And it is those kind of tribes that we learn to flourish from and become thankful to God for when we have them as a part of our circles.

> Blessed is the man who does not walk in the counsel
> of the wicked or stand in the way of sinners or
> sit in the seat of mockers. (Ps. 1:1, NIV)

Over the years, I've been blessed to be a part of different tribes. They have ranged in uniqueness of people, culture, and age. The range has been very wide and vast. Some of my tribes have been comprised from people all over the globe. I guess that's partly why I love to travel and learn about how other people live across the world. I love hearing about the metaphorical trees and climbs from people in other cultures. Trust me, those climbs produce a totally different and unique lifestyle and even a very different format for conducting interviews with God. Our tribes really do play a key component in our development and growth. During my interviews with God, one question that I like to ask him is whether or not I am still yoked up with the right tribe for this particular season in my life. Different tribes are sometimes required for different seasons in our lives.

Some of the greatest tribe members in my life have been people who were able to not only be a confidant, but those who were also great cheerleaders. I have found that every tribe needs an amazing cheerleader. I personally am not much of a natural cheerleader. The rhythm of keeping in step with others and the right words just don't come easily for me. But because I've had some amazing cheerleaders in my own personal tribes, I've learned how to step into that cheerleader position when needed. And I can now give a pretty good bullhorn cheer when someone needs to hear, "Keep climbing!"

When I lost my father as a teenager, it stripped me of one of my best cheerleaders. He was great at supporting me and guiding me up those trees of life. He would challenge me to go to a new height each time I mastered an old height. He'd remind me that each victory turns from the ceiling to the floor and to challenge old habits and perspectives as I pursue and gain knowledge. Those are a lot of lessons from a cheerleader, right? But those are the lessons he taught me daily and modeled before me daily, all while cheering me to go higher and screaming loudly that I could do it! He taught me that I could do anything because with God, all things are possible.

I've been blessed to have several cheerleaders in my tribes. But after my father died, Bishop Johnny Reed became a tremendous cheerleader in my tribe. Even though I didn't really see him that often, maybe at a church conference or a program here and there, he'd always make an intentional point that when he saw me, he'd get suited up and ready to cheer. He'd cheer louder than anyone else whenever he saw me. He'd encourage me to tap into my spiritual gifts. He'd tell me how he sees God using me in a mighty way, and guess what? I'd believe him, and I would always want to grow and learn more about God each time that he cheered!

Bishop Reed even taught me how to trust God for miracles. I'll never forget the night that I received a real, bona fide miracle. This time, Bishop Reed was cheering so loud that he began conducting his own interview with God, in my behalf, for my next position. Bishop Reed was determined that I could go to that next height in the climb.

The setup for the miracle began after I had fallen off a ladder about sixteen feet high and broken my leg. I found myself in the Urgent Care early on a Friday morning, and as I had suspected because I literally heard the bone break when I fell, the x-rays confirmed that my leg was indeed broken. The x-rays showed that I had a clean pretty severe break along my lower fibula. But the swelling was so severe in my leg that the doctor was unable to determine whether or not I was going to need surgery to repair the break, or if they could fit me with a cast and allow it to heal on its own over time. So due to the swelling, I was scheduled to return after the weekend for a follow-up appointment on Monday with an orthopedic specialist.

During that same weekend, I was scheduled to preside over a youth statewide church convocation. Attendees would be fellowshipping together from various churches in our organization from all across the state. I had invited two out-of-state guests to minister during the convocation, and they were booked and scheduled to arrive that same day. I must admit that I was a little nervous about ensuring that everything would work out fine during the convocation. And I guess that it was ultimately my anxiety over this convocation that led me to making the bad decision of climbing that sixteen-foot ladder to clean a ledge in my home. (Cleaning usually helps to calm me down.) In hindsight, of course, this was not a very good decision. However, if it had not been for that fall, I wouldn't have gotten to know God as a miracle worker!

I attended the convocation in pain, wearing a boot and weight bearing only on crutches. I was instructed to perform non-weight-bearing walking and to keep my leg elevated as much as possible. So I literally sat in church the next night, Saturday night, with an elevated wedge and a pillow with my leg propped sideways across the church pew. The vice president had to take over for me all day and night and conduct all the services for the convocation. Then as we were coming to the close of the service, I was asked if I would like to have closing remarks. I graciously thanked everyone for making the convocation such a success, and I said a few other words, and I then turned the floor back over to the pulpit for dismissal. But to my surprise, my cheerleader, Bishop Reed, stood up and began to give a cheer that I will never forget. He said, "God wants to give Sister Stephanie a miracle! God wants to show you that he is still in the miracle-working business." He made that declaration right over the pulpit in front of the entire convocation.

I remembered thinking, *Bishop, are we really about to take a literal faith walk right now at the close of this convocation?* Talk about going out on a limb! Bishop Reed then walked out of the pulpit down to the pew where I was sitting, handed me my crutches, and proceeded to guide me out to the center aisle of the church. He then asked my mother to come on the other side of me and to begin to pray. Next he told my mom to take my crutches and that the two of them were going to support me on each side as we walked up and down that center aisle. Finally, he said that they would hold me up until God healed my broken leg. He told everyone in the church to start praying and believing because on this night, God was going to perform a miracle.

Bishop Reed told me to listen to the prayers and just believe. He began praying openly and sharing very specific testimonies of how he had watched God heal others and reminding the entire church that we today, we still served that same God. Afterward, he began praying a prayer of healing and faith louder and louder, and he began cheering for me to just believe. He said, "Take that first step. God has you. With God, all things are possible! I know that you can activate that faith." He added, "Hear God and know that he will do it. He wants to give you a miracle today."

At that moment, I began to literally take my faith walk. I let go of my mom and Bishop Reed's shoulders, and I began to walk that aisle alone. Next, Bishop Reed instructed my mother to go to me and take that boot off my foot so that I could walk into the fullness of the miracle that God was about to perform. Initially, when she removed the boot and I took those first couple of steps, it was extremely painful. But I kept walking and making those baby steps because my cheerleader was steadily cheering and promising that I would know God today as a miracle worker.

What happened next was simply incredible. I began to feel a burning in my leg that was so hot that I almost couldn't stand it! I thought either I was about to fall down flat and pass out, or God was healing me at that very moment. So guess what? I didn't pass out. Instead, I really believe that it was at that exact moment that God himself performed surgery on my leg! I literally walked out of that service that night without any swelling, without any pain, and without my crutches.

On Monday morning, I showed up at the orthopedist for my appointment without the boot and without the crutches. I shared with the doctor about what had happened on Saturday night. He looked at me and said, "It's good that you're not in pain anymore. It's more than likely due to the fact that swelling has gone away." He went on to say while looking at my first set of x-rays from the Urgent

Care that he wanted to begin my appointment by doing another set of x-rays so as to determine the severity of my fracture. I simply said, "Okay. Let's do what you feel is best."

I knew that the doctor didn't believe that the fracture had healed. I could hardly believe it myself. After all, I am also an occupational therapist as well as a clinical therapist, and I have treated many people with fractures over the course of my career. So I well knew and understood the healing process.

When the doctor returned with my x-rays, he looked at me perplexed. I just smiled. He showed me on the x-rays that were taken that day how my fracture was closed, and it just looked like an old injury. He then showed me the comparison of the x-ray taken on Friday. I was so tickled and almost laughed out loud as he finally said, "I don't have a medical explanation."

For me, the explanation had already occurred on Saturday night.

Jesus is a healer, and he still works miracles! I thank God for Bishop Reed being a part of my tribe. I thank God that he brought Bishop Reed into our interview that Saturday night. And most of all, I thank God that Bishop Reed was not afraid to challenge me to climb higher! He knew that the best fruit was way out on the limb this time. He knew that the risk was worth it and that we can't keep reaching for the low-hanging fruit because God has more for us! So I ask you, *Who is in your tribe* that is cheering for you to keep climbing higher?

12

What Are You Measuring?

How many times have you heard, "What you measure grows"? Your tribe absolutely plays one of the high cards in that growth. Is your tribe helping you to examine and measure your growth in various aspects of your life? What are some of the principles and core values that you and your tribe share? Have you discussed effective tools to measure that progress?

When I was growing up, I used to hate cooking. My grandmother, Bonnie Hill was her name, would bring me in the kitchen and make me help her cook cakes, pies, cookies, and all kinds of delicious baked goods, but I didn't like the work. I liked eating the baked goods, but I didn't enjoy the work. I can remember sitting on the kitchen stool as she instructed me how to measure flour. "Don't shake it in the cup," she would say. "That will pack it, and your measurements will be off." But I found it interesting that while I had to be so specific about how I measured, it seemed that she would just zip right through the process. Not even using some of the same measuring tools that she insisted that I use so precisely. We call that eyeballing it. So why was it that she could eyeball her measurements, and I had to be precise?

The answer was really simple—mastery. Over the years, her skill set had developed such that she was a real master in the kitchen when it came to baking. However, she understood that when you are operating in the role of a teacher, you must not only teach the concepts, but also make sure that the student knows how to make application with the information. I needed to precisely measure and see over and over what a cup of flour looked like in and out of the measuring cup. As a beginner, I needed to learn how to use each measuring tool and understand its purpose. But I also needed to watch her take her hands as the master and measure each of those recipe ingredients just as precisely as mine were that were in the measuring cups.

What I came to realize was that they were both still being measured, just with different tools and from different levels of experience. That's the difference between a novice and a master. They both understand the importance of things having to be measured, but the master is able to transcend across a wide variety of different spectrums and tools.

The same applies for gifts and skill sets. Even though sometimes they are not tangible, they still must be measured. What you measure will grow. It is crucial for us to start identifying skills that are necessary for personal, spiritual, family, and financial development; and then measure how we are growing in each of those areas. A couple of great measuring tools that I have found over the years for measuring those areas of my life are the following: consistency, smart goals, and autopsies.

Consistency

Consistency is one of the most important measuring tools for measuring skill development. It is very easy to take one action and measure how often you perform that action. However, as easy as it is for us to measure consistency, it is also one of the most difficult tools for most of us to utilize. I've found that this measuring tool is underutilized because it is conjoined with discipline. It takes intrinsic discipline or extrinsic coaching to repeat the same actions consistently, no matter how simple the action may be. Think about it, picking up the phone to call and encourage someone is easy to do. But it is also just as easy not to do. There are many things that we are capable of performing in life. Things that naturally fall inside of our skill set and frame of capabilities, but actually doing those things consistently is the difference. And sometimes it's the difference between whether or not we become a master or remain a novice.

Much like I was as the novice baker hating to learn how to cook, sometimes we hate the tool of consistency because of the discipline that it requires. We may even love the reward of the goods that come from our skills and crafts, just like I did from baking, but we struggle with the consistency of taking the necessary actions. They say that most people that have mastered any craft, sport, instrument, or skill have put in more than ten thousand hours of practice. It is virtually impossible to become the expert of anything without discipline and consistency. Is it easy enough to study the same subject one hour per day? Is it easy enough to exercise thirty minutes to an hour five days per week? Is it easy enough to pray three times per day like Daniel? Sure it is. But it's also easy enough not to do.

Once we push past the feelings that consistency is a mundane tool or the excuse that we don't have the time to consistently do things, we'll discover just how truly valuable being consistently consistent is for our lives. Ask yourself, what areas of my life am I willing to measure with consistency? The good news is that once we are using consistency to measure our endeavors, whatever they might be, this tool not only helps us to measure our growth, but it also has a way of crossing barriers that were once stunting and actually preventing our personal growth.

Smart Goals

We've all probably heard the acronym SMART used when discussing how to set goals: *s*pecific, *m*easurable, *a*ttainable, *r*elevant, and *t*ime-based. Sometimes the *A* also stands for *action oriented* or *achievable*. I like using the *A* for action oriented. In the story of my grandmother and I baking together, the master doesn't just allow the novice to sit back and watch, but instead the training is put into action. Achieving even the smallest of goals usually doesn't happen by standing on the sidelines.

At the beginning of each year, I set my personal smart goals. I set goals in four or five life categories, and I write three to four goals in each area. I then make sure to include at least one big audacious goal in each category. I do this because I believe that when I set audacious goals, it ensures that I'll have to continue the interview process with God if I intend to accomplish those goals.

Writing this book was one of my goals that I set at the beginning of 2016. I didn't set a goal to write a best-selling book, nor did I set a goal to write a book that would sell over a million copies. I just simply set a smart goal to write my first book before the end of the year. For me, this was a goal that I had had for over twenty years, but I had never actually written it down as one of my smart goals. Instead, it had been in the back of mind, even in some of my conversations, but it had not been written as a smart goal. By no means are *smart goals* failproof, but they do have a way of guiding us when we take the time to not only write them down, but also revisit them.

I must have started writing this first book over two dozen times or more in the past. The title of the book would be different each time. Even the concept of the book was often different. But each time that I would start to write without fail, I would allow myself to become sidetracked. I'd stop using consistency, or I would tell myself things like, "I'm not good enough to write a book," or "No one wants to hear what I have to say." Actually, I could tell you a laundry list of things that I would say to myself in order to talk myself out of completing the task. But the truth of the matter was that I was just plain afraid. I was afraid of being judged. I was afraid of failing. Sometimes, I was even afraid of succeeding. But once I finally realized that writing this first book was more about moving on to the next stage of my interview process with God, the fear was broken. Finally, for the first time, writing this book was added to my list of SMART goals. And what gets measured grows.

Autopsies

How do you move forward if you don't understand much about your past? We've all heard that doing the same things over and over and expecting different results is insanity, or those who don't learn from their mistakes tend to repeat them. It is these adages and a few others that have made me aware of the need of performing life autopsies. Some people might prefer to call them reviews instead of autopsies. But I believe in really digging in and dissecting even the minute particles. If you don't know what killed your personal growth, then how do you cure it or heal it? How do you determine if there's something that may need to be completely eradicated from your life? I believe that the autopsy is an effective tool for helping to answer these questions. The autopsy is a different measuring tool from the other two tools. The autopsy gives data on where progress was made and where it was blocked.

When I was in undergrad school, we had to work on cadavers in order to learn all the nerve innervations and the origin and insertions of muscles. It was a very difficult course, but one that taught me the human body very well. Dissecting those cadavers gave me insights that I otherwise would not have gleaned about the human body, and it better equipped me as a therapist. I now had a better understanding where to provide points of pressure when working with patients.

I understood why certain splints couldn't cross certain areas of the body so as to not entrap nerves. I had a much greater grasp of *the why*.

I believe that autopsies can be a very effective tool for measuring personal growth. The autopsy examines *the why*. When we are in our interviews with God, we often want him to answer the question why for us. Have you ever found yourself asking, "Why, God? Why did this happen? Why did I lose this person? Why am I so sick? Why haven't I found my soul mate? Why did this or that take place? Why did that door close? Why God? Why, why, why!"

I believe that a lot of times when we ask God *why*, he just lovingly and gently replies with, "*Why not*," or more plainly he's saying to us that if we would just take time to perform the autopsies, then we'll better understand those answers to the *why not*. It is the autopsy that helps us to grow in a very unique way. It is the autopsy that enhances our learning and changes our perspective. It is the autopsy that sets us up and equips us to better understand what to do and what not to do the next time. The autopsy measures a lot of things, including what worked and what didn't work. The autopsy can definitely be a difficult measuring tool to use because it requires us being open to getting to the truth of a lot of our own choices and circumstances present in our lives.

Sometimes when we are performing an autopsy, we may dissect to a point that we discover that this particular association was causing disease in our life, so God had to eradicate that relationship to protect you. Other times we may discover that God had to close a particular door because we had more to offer than that position with that company would have allowed us to give. And yes, there are even those times that although we don't like to admit to them, but God says that this had to happen because we were disobedient. But even in those times, he continues to give us an opportunity to dissect and identify our mistakes and then correct them so that we can grow and become better. The autopsy may be difficult to use, but it is definitely an effective measuring tool and essential for growth.

As we continue to use our measuring tools, we'll eventually find that we are ready to move into the teacher role one day, just like my grandmother was with me when we baked together. It is imperative that we continue to measure our personal growth, spiritual growth, and more. When it comes to spiritual growth, consistency is a great tool to help to measure our fasting, prayer, Bible reading, devotion, and more. SMART goals are great measurement tools that can help to steer us and ultimately deepen and/or broaden our experiences and connection with God. And finally, autopsies can help to measure the results of how we are making choices and application of the spiritual principles that we've learned and the impact that that application is having upon our lives.

What are you measuring?

13

Would You Share Your Interview?

Over the years, I have been blessed to hear some amazing interviews from others. Some may call them stories, but I believe that a lot of our life events are rooted in God saying to the prince of this earth, "Have you considered my child Susie, or have you considered my child Johnny," just as he did with Job in the Bible days. I believe that God looks over our résumés and determines that we are qualified for the assignment, and if we are not yet qualified, then he calls us and says, "I will qualify you through this next experience."

I want to share an interview between God and a friend of mine who we shall call Jennifer. Jennifer is an amazing woman of God who understands that our interviews and our experiences are not just for us to hold on to and never share, but instead our interviews are to be shared so as to help encourage the next person and to let them know that they are not alone. The interview that Jennifer shares below, in her own words, is one that details God calling her for the position of mother.

A Mother's Purpose Fulfilled

Meaning and purpose for my life were fulfilled all at one time when my children were born. I had always wanted to be a mom and a wife. I never had high aspirations for a career. I did not work outside the home, so the children were not given things they wanted all the time, but they were certainly given the material things that they needed. However, meeting the children's needs emotionally was another story.

My husband and I were young, and I in particular was not emotionally or spiritually mature. As the children grew, I was the most involved in their lives. I nurtured, cared for, and chauffeured the children to activities and church while managing the home and spending hours with the middle son, who had identified learning disabilities. The early years of my marriage were hurtful, and I had much resentment toward my husband for his angry outbursts and intimidating behaviors. He was harsh with the children, and I was expected to carry out his rules that at times appeared to be ever changing and unrealistic. I was disillusioned and overwhelmed because I thought that I had to do everything, and everything seemed to be expected of me from my family. So, of course, I attempted to do all and be all. Most of the time during this period in my life, it seemed as if my husband was disconnected from me and the children, that is until he was agitated.

My oldest son was a compliant, quiet, well-mannered studious child, and at seven years of age, he became a Christian and wanted to be baptized. His teachers and friends told me that he would read his Bible to other children on the playground. All through elementary school years, he and his friends would compete on assignments and tests for the highest grades. He loved to visit friends and invite them to church, and he loved to help others. Not only did he love the Lord, but he was also blessed with other talents and gifts. He showed average to above-average potential in baseball and played through the fifteen-year-old leagues. He was also a very good self-taught guitarist, and later, he had lessons that developed and enhanced these talents.

But as I reflect back, the beginning of the sixth grade was difficult and frightening for him because we were unable to afford a private school or to move to another district where many of his friends attended; therefore, he was attending a school with no familiar people at this time in life. Alone at school, his desire to achieve became stunted. He became a quiet child and withdrawn. A lot of times his father would become frustrated with him and would impose punishments that ultimately humiliated him.

I became the buffer between him and his father. During this time, my son was never disrespectful to me or his father, but he became withdrawn and depressed. When he was fifteen, we discovered a wine bottle in his room, and we also realized that he had been smoking. We immediately began to panic. In my opinion, he was restricted often and for far too long. The punishment was out of fear of losing control and, sadly, what others would think of our family. But we convinced ourselves that it was for his good, often shaming him for his actions and behaviors.

We took him to a counselor, who instructed me to back away and allow his father to discipline him because I was not "street smart." I was hurt because I thought that I was insignificant and unappreciated, and I was also angered because I thought that I had failed, and now someone knew that I had failed. My thoughts about the counseling were that I knew what was best and not the counselor. Since I had been the most involved in my son's life, then I knew what was best for him. So since this was how I felt, the counselor told us that there was no need to return. But I remember after that session fearing that I would walk into our son's room and find him hanging from the ceiling dead.

As time went on, our son became more withdrawn. In desperation, without consulting my husband, I took out a loan for him to attend a private school. Soon after starting the new school, he left our home and stayed with a friend from church so as to attend this new school. The friend's mother agreed to let my son stay for a short while, but she said that he would need his own toiletries and money for lunches. My husband forbade me to take these items to him, but I decided to provide them to him in secret. When he returned home after just three short weeks, more rules were applied to him at my husband's instruction, and I had to enforce them. More resentment. More buffering.

But then one morning, I took him to school. I told him goodbye, have a good day, and that I loved him. And it was later that same day that I received a phone call telling me that he had not attended school at all that day. I waited till the afternoon to address the skipping school incident, but to my surprise, he did not return home. I was worried, and his father was angry. I called around to his friends, but no one had any knowledge of where he was. The next morning, my husband did not think that it was necessary to call the police, and he left for work, but I called the police to put out a missing persons report. I was asked had there been trouble at home, and I said no. The officer gave me little hope or encouragement as to the effort that would be given to find my child. He was treating it as a runaway.

I attempted to make life normal for the other two children. I was worried and fearful that my son's life could be in danger and that I would never see him again and that I had no control. I was depressed because my illusion of a fulfilling marriage and perfect children seemed impossible. I was angry that our son and my husband were not acting as I thought they should. I experienced guilt for being so resentful. I was angry and felt that I had failed as a wife and mother and that I had caused these painful circumstances.

The days were endless and the nights even longer. I cried and prayed without ceasing. After eight days of my son being missing, I was exhausted, but yet I was unable to rest or relax. So I went walking around the neighborhood praying and crying. As distraught as I was, on that day, the birds seemed to sing louder. The clouds seemed more beautiful, and the trees and grass were greener for some reason. Everything seemed to fade except the sights and sounds of nature. After a moment of taking it all in, I felt such an overpowering peace, and I began to acknowledge that God was all-knowing and that he was everywhere and that he knew all about my son. So at that moment, I decided to release my son to the Father, and I asked him to protect my child and to guide him. Once I released him to God, my soul began singing "Lord, I Lift Your Name on High," and then eventually my voice began to sing also, and I worshipped.

Although, I was still sad because I missed my child, and I wanted him back into our home and lives. I now had picked up hope, peace, and assurance. I felt a blessed assurance. The next morning, I went out to our back deck to commune with God, and when I did, there sat my missing son, sitting on our back deck. He asked if he could come home. I reached for him, hugged him, and cried tears of joy. My son had returned home!

It was during this period of hard times that a deeper relationship with God developed. I began to understand that the meaning and purpose of my life was not just in being a mother and wife, but it was in praising and serving the Heavenly Father. Motherhood and being a wife were avenues to serve and express the relationship that I have with God. I released God's power in my personal life by asking for forgiveness for my unbelief and my lack of trust in his presence. I thanked God for his patience and grace toward me. Next, I asked my husband for forgiveness for the resentment and anger that I had harbored toward him over the years. And it was after that, that in turn, the process of my forgiving him began.

I began to allow God to renew my mind and create a right spirit in me. One of the ways that I did this was by mentally observing my motivations and my behaviors. I realized that throughout some of my circumstances, my goals had been to relieve my pain, and that was not what was needed. So I changed my motivations and my focus. I focused on "doing unto the Lord," not just relieving my emotional pain.

Behaviorally, I set boundaries with myself by recognizing the things that I was responsible for and the things that I was not. I also started identifying what I could control and what I could not control. Emotionally, I allowed myself to feel emotions, even anger when it was to right a wrong. I learned to express my emotions appropriately so that resentment could not take root and cause damage to me or others.

I began to find security in knowing God and trusting that he would meet all my needs. I also realized that my husband was not responsible, nor was he equipped to meet all my emotional needs of significance and security. Over the next few months, I learned to verbalize my needs and desires as well as my likes and dislikes to my husband. No longer was I expecting him to know my inner thoughts and feelings if I did not express them. It was during this time in my life that as I committed to doing the work required to build a lasting relationship with God that I began experiencing joy in the Lord and commitment to his will, even in the face of adversity.

As I came to realize that my son and his father were responsible for the dynamics of their relationship and not me, I began to release control and let God do his work in them. I began trusting that God would make something beautiful out of my son's life. In other words,

I acknowledged God's ownership of my son and released my son to God's grace, mercy, and love. Although the heartaches and tensions would continue throughout my son's teen years, there was much that I learned, and more lessons remained to be taught.

God spoke clearly to me through these trials that my work would be to bring hope to the hopeless, stand alongside those that are in despair, and to share the truth that would set people free. I was called to help people cope with depression, anxiety, and anger. God had a specific plan for my life, and I began to listen to him unfold it. This plan involved me returning to college and preparing to be a servant. Today, I am a counselor, and my desire is to be faithful to God's word and his assignments for my life.

Sometimes, there are still trials that occur with my children even as they are now adults, and sometimes I momentarily default to worry, depression, and anger. But hallelujah, God softly and tenderly grabs my attention. I repent and I praise him for who he is and who he will always be. I thank him for all that he does and will do. I rest in the shelter of his arms. I gain strength for the next journey. I soar in his freedom.

Jennifer's interview is a beautiful expression of someone being called for a position that they may have thought initially that they were not ready to take. I love how she shares that it was when she began to let God speak during her interview, things began to change.

Isn't it amazing that he can even bring nature into our interviews to share if he wants to? His charts and spec sheets are from the very foundation of the world. They are like no other. He can bring creation into the interview as his whiteboard to remind us that he still owns everything, and that it is his word and his recommendations that determine the final say on our assignment. I really wholeheartedly believe that in life, we all have an interview or two that needs to be shared. *Are you willing to share yours?*

14

What Really Matters?

I can still remember my wedding day most days as if it was yesterday, even though it has been over twenty years now. I remember the nervousness, excitement, joy, and so many more emotions that I was surged with on that day. It actually rained during the early morning, and then the sun came out a few hours just before the ceremony! My aunt said that those early showers and then the beaming of the sun were a sign of blessings. It indeed was a beautiful and amazing spring day as I, this young bride, presented herself unto her groom.

We had been through a lot to get to this big day. But the biggest battle came when our caterer decided to skip town without anyone being aware. Not only did he skip town, but he also took our deposit for the country club room and over half of the total cost of the reception, and just to add a little more insult to injury, he double-booked our wedding date at the country club before skipping town. So not only was our money gone, but we were also left without a venue to host the reception one month before our big day. (Not many people even know this part of our story.) With over five hundred guests attending on that day, barely anyone other than our family knew about the battle that we had been facing concerning our wedding reception.

Funny how God has a way of not letting you look like what you are going through! So what do you do when there are no other venues available, you don't' have the funds to really pay for another reception, and you have only one month to pull it all together? I tell you what—you call on the name of your heavenly father to come see about you. And that is exactly what I did after I had a visit to the emergency room for heart arrhythmias. Yes, it took me a minute to realize that I needed to call on him, but I eventually got there.

As I began sitting in my chair across from God having yet another interview with him, I began dominating the conversation. I started giving him a laundry list of my so-called qualifications. After all, I had stayed faithful, pure, a woman of integrity. I had worked in the church, and I had been a witness for him. So the only question that I wanted God to answer at this moment was, why do you keep allowing these devastations to occur in my life? Why, God?

I bet you are thinking, "Oh no, tell me you didn't!" Tell me you did not get angry and sassy with God? But yes, I did. I came into that interview as so many people have gone into job interviews, and

I acted as if I were in charge. Looking back on it, I am surprised that God didn't check me like he did Job. "Job where were you when I laid the earth's foundation? Tell me, if you understand" (Job 38:4, NIV). But instead of chastising me, he allowed me to finish my rant, and then he nicely gave me another opportunity to re-interview. Have you ever messed up an interview, but the employer allowed you to come back and try again? Well, that's what happened to me with God during this time in my life.

In the next couple of days, I returned for my interview. I took an entirely different posture and approach. Instead of ranting and insisting that God come to my rescue, I humbled myself and began to listen to what he said mattered for this particular assignment, or should I say position. I took to heart the résumé and qualifications that he shared that he was looking for in order to fill this position. I listened to him tell me about the bonuses that would be gained if I was willing to follow his job description and stop creating my own. I really listened, and then I accepted his guidance. The greatest lesson that I was taught during this time in my life was how to understand the difference between what was my business and what was God's business.

It was now about two weeks before my wedding day, and I still didn't have a venue to hold my reception. But I was determined to not feel defeated. I kept saying to myself that even if I couldn't have a reception, what really mattered was the fact that I was marrying the man that God had ordained for my life. I kept telling myself to hold on to the things that really mattered. As I went to work on this day, one of my coworkers came over to me while I was treating one of my hand patients. She asked me whether or not I had found a new venue for our reception. She began to share how badly she felt for me over how this caterer had ruined our big day. She lamented on and on about how awful this was and how horrible she felt, but I kept telling myself that it would be okay.

After hearing my coworker lament on and on, my patient that I was treating at the time began to ask me if I would share with her the details as to what had happened. So I told her that I didn't mind talking about it, and I began to share my story. She expressed her heartfelt regrets for me and told me not to give up, that things would somehow work out. I honestly didn't know how things would work out because I had called every venue within a forty-mile radius of our wedding site, and I had come up empty. But for some reason, I found just a little more assurance in her words. Somehow, things would work out.

About two days later, that same patient who had told me that somehow things would work out, returned for her next appointment. She told me that she was so excited to get here today and that she could hardly wait to talk to me. She said to me, "I have good news!" She continued on by saying, "I was so upset about what had happened to you that I spoke to my husband about your situation, and I asked him if he could do anything to help fix this for you." She went on to explain that her husband was the chief of police in the same city where my wedding was to occur. She said, "My husband felt so bad that he called in a few favors, and the police department wants to give you their private banquet hall for your reception, free of charge." She said, "It's beautiful. It has a huge gorgeous fireplace as the focal point, beautiful chandeliers, and a full chef's kitchen."

I could hardly believe what she was telling me. I accepted the blessing and began thanking her and God. This was incredible! After I came out of being in awe of God, my thoughts then turned to the fact that I still needed a caterer. What about the catering services? Where could I find a caterer on such short notice to cater my reception with my remaining limited budget? Well, I didn't have to find that either. My aunt stepped in and convinced a friend of hers, who was a professional chef and caterer, to drive two hours to my hometown and cater the entire reception for only the cost of the food. We literally planned my wedding reception within about one week of the actual wedding.

The real reason that I chose my wedding story to share is not because of the challenges that I had to face and the lessons that I learned from those challenges, but I share this story mainly because of the serenade that my husband and I received at the wedding reception. It is the words of that serenade that have carried me for some twenty-plus years each time I interview with God. The words of the song simply said, "Remember, only what you do for Christ will last."

I don't know if it was how she sang the song or because of everything that we had been through in order to have a wedding reception, but whenever I have challenges or struggles in my life, I still think back to those words: "Remember, only what you do for Christ will last." Those words help me to center my thoughts on what really matters. When situations and circumstances feel critical in my life, those few words from that song help me to prioritize and make decisions once I've asked and answered the question, *what really matters?*

It is that thought that I want to leave with you as I close this book. We will all continue to have interviews with God throughout our lives. He may interview us from different relationships inside of his deity. Sometimes, our interview may be with the father; other times it will be with the Holy Spirit or with his son Jesus. But no matter when or at what point the interview comes in our life, all that we have to do is to stay focused on what really matters. And at the end of the day, the only thing that really matters is that we "remember, only what we do for Christ will last."

I believe that we will all have a final interview one day. It will be an incredible interview. An interview that will be the interview of all interviews and that will place us into our ultimate position. This won't be a position like any other position. This position is one that is so incredible "that no eye has seen, no ear has heard, and no human mind has conceived the things God has prepared for those who love him" (1 Cor. 2:9, NIV). This position is full of wonderful benefits and bonuses. I get excited just thinking about some of the amazing bonuses that we will have: streets of gold, gates of pearl, jeweled crowns, and wonderful mansions for housing.

It is that interview, as we are standing before God as a beautiful bride, adorned and ready to present herself to her groom, that we will truly understand that what really matters is hearing God say, "You have interviewed well. Great job. Well done!" What an incredible interview that will be! It will be the most amazing **Interview with God**.

About the Author

Stephanie Hill Nchege is a unique and refreshing blend of therapist, coach, motivational speaker, and cheerleader. Her desire is that her life models the passage "I am made all things to all men, that I might by all means save some" (1 Cor. 9:22). She is a wife of over twenty years to Ike Nchege, mother of two amazing boys, Chetachi and Onyeka, and professionally, she has been a board certified and licensed therapist for over twenty years. She is also a master's level clinical therapist and a certified life coach. Stephanie has spoken at conferences throughout the United States. She stands firmly on the premise that in this world, we can make a difference, one life at a time.

Stephanie is the owner of Finally Living Coaching where she coaches clients through the process of how to unlock their God-ordained vision and purpose. She diligently works professionally to meet people where they *are* and render unto them service that may help enable them to go where they *dream*! Her clients and audiences have often referred to her as a "breath of fresh air." At the end of each day, Stephanie Hill Nchege just wants to make sure that she has lived a day worth counting, a day that has helped someone else, a day that honors God.

CPSIA information can be obtained
at www.ICGtesting.com
Printed in the USA
BVHW03s2308150218
508098BV00001B/93/P